Landscape as Spirit

Creating a
Contemplative
Garden

Landscape as Spirit

Spirit

Creating a Contemplative Garden

Martin Hakubai Mosko, ASLA
and Alxe Noden

Foreword by Eido Shimano Roshi

WEATHERHILL

an imprint of Shambhala Publications, Inc.

Horticultural Hall

300 Massachusetts Avenue

Boston, Massachusetts 02115

www.shambhala.com

First edition, 2003
Third printing, 2007

Printed in China
® This edition is printed on acid-free paper that meets the
American National Standards Institute Z39.48 Standard.
Distributed in the United States by Random House, Inc.,
and in Canada by Random House of Canada Ltd

ISBN 978-0-8348-0538-5

Library of Congress Cataloging-in-Publication data available

To all our teachers

Contents

Foreword

Martin Mosko is, first of all, a wonderful human being. Second, he is a Buddhist scholar and a Zen monk. He has been practicing *zazen* for thirty years; *zazen* energy permeates his life. And third, he is a gardener. He obviously considers the creation of a garden a spiritual practice. His gardens are nothing but an expression of his spiritual being.

In his creative effort, Martin includes Tibetan views, Japanese aesthetics, and Chinese philosophy. He understands the energy of heaven and earth the way Native Americans do. The garden Martin shares with us is a condensation of the universe. Though we cannot point to a particular aspect, somehow it invites us to contemplation.

In Kyoto there is a Zen temple called Ryoan-ji, famous for its rock garden. Countless visitors sit down on the deck facing that rock garden. Unconsciously, they go into a deeper state of mind, breathe with the space, unite with its utmost simplicity. We cannot point out anything in particular about it; yet this is what makes the garden so special.

I had known for a long time Trungpa Rinpoche and Kobun Otogawa Roshi, both of whom were influential in Martin's practice. In the summer of 2002, Kobun Otogawa Roshi suddenly passed away in Switzerland. It was shocking news. I went to Boulder, Colorado, to conduct a funeral service with Trungpa Rinpoche's son, the Sakyong Mipham Rinpoche, at his request. It was then I first met Martin in this lifetime. The more we talked, the more we were amazed at how much we had in common.

Among many teachers he mentions in his preface is Isamu Noguchi. Though I never mentioned this to Martin, Mr. Noguchi and I lived in the same building for over five years. When I decided to move there, Mr. Noguchi's presence helped me to be accepted as a resident of that cooperative in Manhattan. Thus, Mr. Noguchi and I had lots of opportunities to discuss stone, gardens, and Zen.

This is how the garden mandala unfolded: Martin appeared to maintain the bridge between Noguchi-san, Trungpa Rinpoche, Kobun Otogawa Roshi, and me.

—Eido Shimano Roshi

The mountain sits with

undifferentiated,

unlimited mind.

White clouds encircle the

White Peak.

Rain falls to the ground

Creating rivulets, brooks,

cascades, and pools.

The eastern sun arises.

Flowers bloom in space,

the color of rainbows.

The wind chases the dragons

along the sage's path.

Preface and Acknowledgments

Thirty years ago I met Juan Garcia, the gardener at the Soledad Mission in California. The mission was a beautiful and forgotten place; many people thought it was in ruins, and it was rare to see a visitor on the grounds. I lived next door, seeking quiet to recover from a painful bout of shingles. I walked to the mission's garden every morning and spent the day painting and writing poetry. One day Juan told me that his left foot had swollen so badly that he couldn't continue to take care of the gardens. He offered to teach me to maintain the place so that I could become the mission gardener. He taught me tree pruning, soil preparation, and care of perennials and roses. Eventually I became his successor.

Now, thirty years and many gardens later, my left foot is swollen and I have difficulty walking. It is time for me to pass along what I have learned on the path of the garden builder, as Juan once did with me.

Founding Marpa & Associates

After I left Soledad Mission I worked on a biodynamic farm and as gardener for the archbishop of Martinique. When I moved to Boulder in 1974 with my wife and young daughter, I started my own garden business, naming it Marpa, after an eleventh-century Tibetan who was both a farmer and a Buddhist master—one of the great translators of texts from Pali to Tibetan.

Marpa is said to have been responsible for the introduction of weeding into Tibetan agriculture. He

traveled by foot three times to India (the last undertaken when he was more than eighty years old) through difficult and dangerous terrain to study with Naropa, and to bring tantric texts back to Tibet. He was also an important part of his community and an ordinary family householder.

Much of my life has been inspired by Marpa. Like him, I've tried to combine daily life with family, business, and complete dedication to my Buddhist practice.

Creating Sacred Spaces

A garden is an artistic expression tapped into the fundament of the creative process: living things. Throughout the world, people re-create in their surroundings their ideas of perfection and natural beauty. The garden is filled with the mystery, the myth of creation. It is a place of peace, solace, healing, and inspiration.

But making a garden is more than art; it is a spiritual practice. It is a process of relating in a compassionate way to the living land, to the sentient beings that inhabit it, to the rocks and plants and earth that occupy the space. Design at its best mediates between the human beings that designate a piece of property as their own through a human legal system and the ecosystem that pre-exists that ownership and will outlast it.

I have built gardens not simply as compelling spaces but as landscapes that shape the lives of those who see them and live in them. From the imagination springs a

system that can and does affect the internal experience of others. So I try to understand both the owners and their property, and work with a sense of responsibility to the ultimate product. I try to sense deeply the spirit of the land, and design with an attitude of respect toward it.

This means more than, for example, planting xeriscape plants (which use less water) in dry climates, or making sure that views aren't obscured by the trees I install. Instead, this attitude goes deeper, involving an understanding of both what is possible in a certain place, and what is responsible in that place. How to fill a space with beauty and magic, while respecting the land and its inhabitants? That has been my life's search.

My Teachers

I have been blessed with a few extraordinary teachers and been influenced and shaped by many others.

Chogyam Trungpa Rinpoche, a venerable Tibetan Buddhist teacher, asked me to build Japanese-style gardens on an American scale. He encouraged me to understand the essence of the Japanese aesthetic, and how that relates to American stature and ways of sitting and walking and entertaining. To make an authentic transmutation was his mandate. This led me to the use of large stones and heavy equipment in order to accomplish the scale of my gardens. He is also my *vajrayana* master and has illuminated my fundamental view.

Another formative teacher was Kobun Otogawa Roshi. He was a Japanese Zen master who had me do the practice for many years of "setting vision." For me, this was the practice of looking at an existing landscape, then overlaying that with a vision of what could be there. The expanded form of this practice was to look at existing social and cultural forms, overlaying these patterns with visions of how we can each live together with others happily, and then understand how to manifest this in the garden. He brilliantly led me through three years of retreat and then sent me to his elder brother—my lineage master Hojosama Tenzan Keibun Roshi. Hojosama asked me to help care for the temple garden.

Working with him day by day I began to learn the essence of the Japanese garden. One late autumn day I came into the tearoom and told him that I had looked everywhere in the garden but could find nothing to do. He said, "See the maple leaves on the ground? You must sweep them up every day." I remembered enjoying walking on colorful aspen leaves and listening to them crunch, so I asked him why I must sweep them up. "Then we can appreciate each day the newly fallen leaves," he replied. Once he wrote a calligraphy: "Even Heaven's horse must polish himself every day." The deeper teaching is that garden building and spiritual practice are really about the perfection of character, little by little, moment by moment, breath by breath.

And there were my parents. My mother taught me everything I know about aesthetics, as well as music, a love of nature, and about kindness. She understood that what really keeps us fully alive is beauty, and that beauty is a precious gift we must constantly offer. My father was my constant support and inspiration, and my greatest fan.

The people who helped to give birth to each garden were also my teachers. Particular artists without whom the gardens would have been very different are: Chester Simmons, Fiona Lloyd, Jay Markel, Sean Acuna, Scott Deemer, and Dante Ortiz.

I have also been influenced very much by the work of Isamu Noguchi, master of stone and space; as well as Cézanne, who studied mountains and light; Monet, who focused on water and its relation to mind; Mark Rothko, who examined vibration and space; Joseph Albers and the Yale art and linguistics schools of the 1960s; as well as many masters of *sumi-e* painting.

My orientation to landscape architecture specifically has been influenced by the work of Dan Kiley, James Rose, Garrett Eckbo, Thomas Church, and recently by Robert Murasi, Peter Weiss, and Shunmyo Masuno.

My roots sink into many different soils, some continents and centuries apart, but they sustain a single tree. The tree is grateful to the roots that give it life and direction.

—MARTIN HAKUBAI MOSKO

The Ground

Garden as Mandala

A contemplative garden is a place to discover the magic of who we are and how we join with the world around us. By engaging and delighting the senses, it brings the mind to attention, to a fuller awareness not only of the natural world, but also of the sacred that inhabits the space. It is landscape as spirit.

Landscape architecture has often abandoned this dimension of garden-making. The aim of much of today's design is to create an elegant solution to a specific set of problems. This might involve environmental and urban planning, arranging pedestrian traffic flow on a campus, softening the lines of a structure, or the integration of that structure with its surroundings. These are worthwhile achievements, but they are not the reason for making a garden.

Martin Mosko's journey has been an exploration of the subject of the garden as a creation where the spirit can play. He has been building gardens for almost thirty years, developing his own style and his own understanding of what the creation of a garden is about on a spiritual level. Once he tried to explain his point of view to some of his students in a park design class. He asked them to imagine that they had been sent to Earth, where they would see the wonders of the planet: its rivers, mountains, lakes, oceans, flowers, and trees. When they return home, how would they re-create the Earth's splendor in miniature, distilling the essence of its spirit?

A contemplative garden is one beyond mere style.

This is the garden builder's mandate. The motivation for creating the garden is more than a search for something to please the eye. The question is how to use a meditative understanding to organize and transform a space.

What does it mean to create a contemplative garden? Thinking of garden design in these terms means to go beyond considerations of style. A contemplative space can look like a Japanese Zen garden of raked sand and rock, or like an English country garden overflowing with flowers and greenery. These descriptions only tell you what flavor the garden has, or what culture has informed its design, not whether it has that extra dimension of spirit and magic. To understand the creation of a garden at this level, the designer must have another, higher paradigm in mind.

One name for this paradigm is a mandala. This term is used to describe both a metaphysical space as well as the physical representation of that space. The mandala is that higher principle, beyond style, which is the basis for the garden infused with spirit.

Humans seem innately drawn to the mandala, which is usually an outer circle filled with inner squares, with entrances and exits. Psychoanalyst C. G. Jung believed it was universally recognizable and a part of the collective unconscious.

We have been building mandalas for nearly as long as records allow us to know. The shape of may have

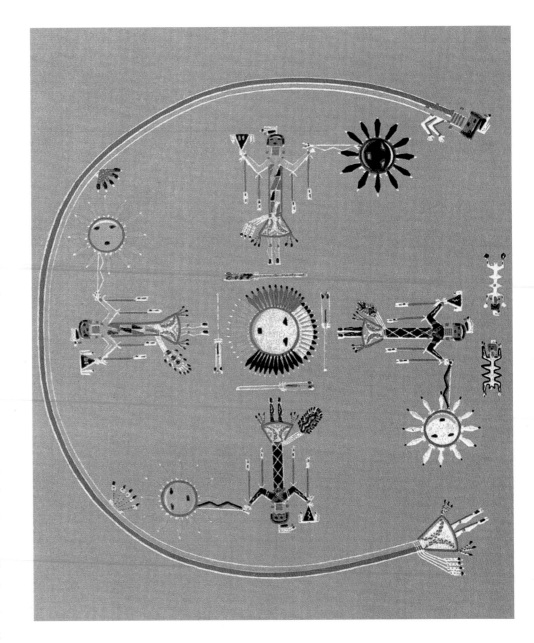

6 evolved from ritual circles used in the earliest religious rites.[1] The ziggurats made in Mesopotamia five thousand years ago took the shape of a mandala. We can see mandalas in the rose windows in European cathedrals.

Mandalas began to be used to invoke some higher sense of being in the person viewing them or entering them. Native Americans use mandala representations of the cosmos as part of their healing ceremonies. Among the Navajo these take the form of sandpaintings which show the balance of all nature's forces.[2] A Tibetan teacher describes a mandala as a space which "integrates shapes and colors with the elements and the points of the compass in a symmetrical representation of the harmony of the universe."[3]

What this book means by "mandala" is any organization of garden space that consciously invites and summons invisible energies, whether they are called angels or deities or Buddha nature. The physical shape this takes does not matter. The mandala is the space in which the inner world of the self meets the outer world; it is where absolute reality meets and is expressed as form.

A garden mandala overlays an existing energetic pattern. The existing pattern is the topography, the way the wind blows through, the way the plants have adapted to conditions, the way the drainage works. We might call this the "relative system." In making the garden, we

Facing page: A garden based on a traditional idea of a mandala, a circle with entrances and exits.

Left: A Tibetan painted mandala.

are overlaying this with a design that reflects the "ultimate system." The ultimate is reality as we experience it in meditation, the clear perception of the way all things, seen and unseen, exist. It is marked by balance, harmony, and calm. The best design merges relative and ultimate so that they are not separate, they interpenetrate and are interdependent. When this merger occurs, a contemplative space arises. This joining of inner and outer realities is the most profound aspect of a garden as mandala.

There are other means of creating mandalas, so why do people create gardens? Because in our quest for order and pattern, in our attempt to embrace chaos through meaning, we turn to the most material element possible, the earth. The Native Americans and the Tibetans use sand to make a mandala. A gardener uses rock, water, plants, paths, and light. Unlike a sand mandala, which is an aid to visualizing a perfect world, a garden mandala is magic itself, bringing blessings to and infusing all who enter it with its spirit. This enables the well-made garden to become a trigger for a contemplative state, a means of invoking a different state of mind in the viewer.

In our usual cement-covered environments, designed for efficiency and utility rather than ease or inspiration, it is difficult to enter or remain in a state of calm awareness. Our minds are rushed and scattered as we ride the bus, drive the roads, or navigate the corri-

*Before (right) and after (facing page):
A garden mandala overlays an
existing energetic pattern.*

dors of our work spaces. A garden offers other possibilities. If it is only decoration of the architecture or a means to direct the flow of traffic, then it does no more for us than any other structure. But if it is made with the intention of creating a contemplative space, if it arises from the right state of mind, and with the right understanding of the materials used and how they relate to one another and the overall plan, then a garden becomes a living shrine. The harried, unhappy mind has no encouragement in such a place. It relaxes into a state of sanity.

From a garden design point of view, the mandala is an organized collection of metaphors made up of the elements of the garden: mountains, rivers, ponds, verandas, grottoes, gazebos, valleys, meadows, forests, and so on. They are metaphors because they are more than the materials or assemblages themselves. Each element represents some aspect of a deeper mind, just as colored sand poured into a pattern can stand for a deity in a Tibetan mandala.

Finding and using the correct design metaphors for a contemplative garden require a preparation of mind that is more than simply sitting down with pen and paper. There is a direct correspondence between the outer mandala of the garden and what we might call the inner mandala of the body and mind. The garden one creates depends on the state of the inner mandala. If the designer has a busy and distracted mind, or cannot feel

Facing page: Magic can occur when all the elements are present and balanced.

Left: Each element represents some aspect of a deeper mind.

the balance of the elements inside his or her own body, a busy and distracted garden results. Nothing in it is ever quite right, and the viewer cannot feel intuitively at rest. If instead the gardener designs from a meditative mind, a quiet mind and clear body, the garden is balanced and healing.

When this state of mind is made manifest, both the process of creation and the object created are contemplation. When a good calligrapher begins with the meditative mind, drawing characters is a contemplative process, and the finished calligraphy is a contemplative object. It is the same for designing a garden: a contemplative garden arises from a meditative mind, the process of design and building is a contemplation, and when finished, the garden becomes an object of contemplation.

There are many metaphorical systems incorporating the elements that can be used to organize the garden. Undoubtedly there are as many ways to conceptualize space as there are people. Certain systems, though, have developed in both Oriental and Occidental cultures for centuries and have been used repeatedly in garden design. Of these, three are used throughout this book.

First is the Heaven/Earth/Man system, which considers the garden a space in which each of these parts must be represented. In this system, used widely in

The natural hierarchy of Heaven, Earth, and Man is expressed through the relationship of the materials in the garden.

Japanese flower arranging schools and in other schools of thought about cosmological organizing principles, each of these parts must be present in a balanced way to bring the garden together. The Heaven element is the tallest, towering over the others as the protection, the roof, and representing a limit of the unreachable. Earth is the base, low and powerful and spreading. Man exists between these elements, resting on but rising higher than Earth, but not so far as Heaven. This natural hierarchy is expressed through the relationship of the three parts and is made manifest by the materials that represent each part.

Second is the five-element system, based on Earth, Water, Fire, Air, and Space. In this system, Earth is the fixed element. The Water element connects and eases. The Fire element is the energy of the sun. Air can also be thought of as wind, or moving energy. Space, the background to all things manifest, is symbolized by the empty quality in the garden. Wonderful magic can occur when all these elements are present and balanced.

Finally, on the most esoteric and perhaps most important level, materials in the garden can represent the three aspects of enlightened mind. First is the Absolute, the wisdom nature of enlightenment. The Manifest is the form we can perceive and contact through our senses. It is enlightenment appearing to living beings. The Connection is communication, the link between the Absolute and the Manifest, the compassion of an enlightened being.[4] Again, the garden is incomplete unless it contains all three aspects.

The Heaven/Earth/Man metaphor helps to understand the physical relationships among the garden's materials, the five element system relates to the energetic properties of the materials, and the Absolute/Communication/Manifest metaphor is a means to understand the metaphysical relationship among the materials.

It is critical to remember that each of these metaphorical systems is only a means to interpret or understand a mandala. A garden begins with a poetic vision, not an intellectual concept. Once the vision arises, these metaphorical systems are useful in helping to use the materials of the garden, and in understanding how those materials relate to one another, how balance is achieved. Any material can be any part of these systems. For example, in a three-stone rock arrangement, one upright boulder can be Heaven, a flat, low-lying boulder can be Earth, and an intermediate boulder can be Man. Just as easily, though, the Man part of this system could be represented by a dwarf tree that is taller than the Earth rock and shorter than the Heaven rock. In a garden that contains Earth, Fire, Air, and Space, there will be no sense of completion without Water also being represented. If there are restrictions on the use of water due to cost or other considerations, then a dry

*The Absolute is the
wisdom nature of
enlightenment.*

The home is part of the energetic system of the garden.

streambed of small cobblestones could become the Water element and create the necessary balance. The water in a pond can actually be the Earth element if it is juxtaposed with a boulder as the Man element and a tall tree as Heaven. The meaning of the materials themselves is entirely mutable. What is important is the metaphor and how the materials are used to complete it.

The garden mandala must also take account of the dwelling of the people who own it. The home doesn't exist on its own, it exists in an environment. By its orientation to that environment it creates its own energetic field, or feeling, which becomes part of the garden's pattern. The metaphors used in the garden should be appropriate to the house and congruent with its environment.

Garden design teaches the laws of nature: it reacquaints us with the gross level of gravity, masses, balance, and the nature of water to seek a level. It assists us in mindfulness, since the gardener must be aware of the health of the living materials of the design, and plan for their well-being. It teaches an appreciation for the unseen, in dealing with the energy of the land and with the power of the earth itself.

Garden design can also be a path of transformation. The designer must become familiar with the inner mandala, the inner workings of the body and mind, in order to create a contemplative space. In the garden, con-

stants are understood through change. The flow of seasons and the growth and death of the plants are the flow of life. Yet the relationships among the elements of the mandala remind us of the unchanging nature of ultimate reality, which is experienced both internally and externally. The process of visualizing and creating a contemplative garden offers an opportunity to explore these dimensions of reality in oneself.

This is a book about building contemplative gardens, but it is also about creating a contemplative life. This does not mean living alone in seclusion or rejecting the world outside the garden walls. It means looking deeply into one's own mind to discover its nature, its balance, and its harmony, and using that understanding in re-creating the environment outside yourself.

The
Path

Making
Magic
Happen

Earth

Everything that we experience is a dialogue between ordinary reality, which constantly changes with growth and decay, and some greater reality, which is unchanging, absolutely itself. The play between these two is expressed in a garden through the materials used. Each material—rock, plants, water, and soil—must be used effectively, to create something that is not only beautiful but also sacred. In addition, each material must be used in proper proportion and balance with all the others.

Stones (and mountains, which are algorithms of stone) are the Earth element of the garden. They have been part of the symbolism and mythology of even primitive societies. For some, stones have represented a deity.[1] A stone might be worshipped alone, or arranged in a geometrical pattern, as at Stonehenge. In the Old Testament, Jacob uses a stone for a pillow, then has a dream in which God reveals himself to Jacob. When he awakes, Jacob takes the stone, symbolic of his meeting with the ultimate, and sets it upright as a pillar. One of the holiest sites in Islam is the Kaaba, the black stone in Mecca.

A stone may also represent the unchanging nature of a person. Many folk customs hold that stones, precious or otherwise, are containers of the life-form: the ancient Germans believed that their spirits lived in their tombstones.[2] One of Jung's followers believes that the "alchemical stone" combines the symbols of the deity and the individual, so that the stone symbolizes the

Rocks are mountains;

mountains are rocks.

Stones must harmonize with all the other materials in the garden.

mystical experience of God within one's own soul, the part of the self that can never be lost or dissolved.[3]

While stone, boulders, and mountains in the garden call forth earlier traditions into the present, they also resonate with very modern sensibilities. No one who creates a garden has to have the appeal of stone explained. People seem drawn to rocks instinctively, whether because they are reacting to deep psychological influences, or because they consciously identify stones as sacred.

Rocks are more than symbols of the unchanging, the ultimate reality, the deities, and the deities of ourselves. In a contemplative garden, they *are* those things. This understanding changes our approach to choosing rocks. A gardener cannot look at a rock and try to figure out what it might stand for; he or she must look at a rock and understand what it is.

For the garden builder, stone is a fundamental building material. Boulders create structure—a conscious or unconscious geometry or organization. They are the unchanging element of the garden. Once they are set, the energetic personality of the garden is set. This understanding is deeply rooted in the Japanese gardening tradition. The oldest known Japanese book on gardening, *Sakuteiki (Records of Making Gardens)*, reminds the gardener that all the rock, no matter what role it plays, "must be set powerfully."[4]

A rock can embody a meaning such as "Buddha rock" or "attendant rock," or a quality, such as vulnerability, friendliness, generosity, or compassion. A rock can also be a part of a larger composition where it is carefully pieced with other rocks to embody a meaning or a quality, or to make a form, such as a dragon or a lion. Whether alone or set in groups, rocks will find expression through form, gesture, and relationships.

Rock setting is limited by site conditions, the people you work with, equipment, and the weather, among other factors. Learning to juggle these conditions and linking the stone with the design is partly intuitive, partly learned.

Two teachers heavily influenced Mosko's rock work: Katsushita Yamazaki and Yoshinori Murakami. Yamazaki Sensei came to the United States and worked with Marpa for a year. He was an older man who came from a school of rigorous apprenticeship, and would teach mostly by shouting "Damay! Damay!" which means "No, never!" He was always finding fault, but in an instructive way. After shouting, he would demonstrate how to do the task correctly.

Yamazaki Sensei transmitted centuries-old techniques. His designs were consciously part of a tradition, a lineage. He was a great scholar of stone setting, and every stone that he set and every garden he designed and built was related to hundreds of gardens he was intimately aware of and garden designers he knew, some of whom had taught him. When he set a

Rocks are the bones of

the garden.

Stone is an expression of something fundamental, of the Absolute.

stone it spoke to every stone set in the history of Japan, which he knew thoroughly.

When he set stones he rarely used power equipment. He used a tripod, chainfall (a gear-ratio pulley), and chains around the stones. This makes for a very slow and deliberate process. He would direct the crew to stand one man at each leg of the tripod, then he would lift the stone and move it a few feet from where it stood. Then the tripod would have to be reset for the next movement toward its final placement.

Among the many things Mosko learned from Yamazaki Sensei was the sheer difficulty of moving stones. This made him consider quite carefully and from the very first how many stones would be used in a garden and how they would be placed. Using these ancient methods makes one much more deliberate and mindful.

Mosko's second Japanese teacher was Yoshinori Murakami, who came and lived with him in America. Murakami Sensei was much more open to unconventional ways of doing things. He was used to working with cranes, and viewed tripods as remnants of the antiquated past. However, he also started a job knowing the number of stones he would use.

He would choose the large stones, and set them first. All his large stones were set to form a relationship among them, even though they might be very far apart. Then the midsize and smaller stones were set, creating groupings with the larger stones. These groupings

related to other groupings. Each stone and group had its own definite physicality and identity, and expressed itself in relation to the others.

One of the most important things Mosko learned from Murakami Sensei was the way to assess rocks to understand their centers. Each boulder's vertical axis relates to the horizontal, and where the two meet is the center of the stone. Once you find the center, you can understand the degree to which the stone stands straight or leans in one direction or another. This is important in determining both the character of the stone and its relation to the ground.

No matter how the stone is used, it must be balanced with all the other stones and with the other elements of Water, Fire, Air, and Space. To find the proper way to set the various stones together one must work from an understanding of the physical, energetic, and metaphysical relationships between the materials rather than just from the specific shapes of the rock forms. This is the only way to achieve the critical balance between the rocks and the other elements in an arrangement that is simple, elegant, and beautiful. This philosophy is also expressed in *Sakuteiki,* in a section titled "Secret Teachings on Setting Stones," where the text tells us:

> Choose a particularly splendid stone and set it as the Main Stone. Then, following the request of the first stone, set others accordingly.[5]

The Heaven rock looms above and behind the Man rock, which connects to the low Earth rocks.

When the rocks are set, the energetic pattern
of the garden is determined.

Clearly the "felt" energy of the stones dictates their arrangement. There is further guidance to rock setting in *Sakuteiki,* such as the requirement that if there are stones that appear to flee the main grouping, that others should be seen to give chase, and that upright and reclining boulders should balance one another.[6] This advice is purely stylistic, but it can be helpful for the novice.

The practical difficulty for the garden designer is how to arrive at an arrangement that feels balanced and solid, that creates the proper sacred connection between the earth and the people in the garden.

One way to achieve this is through the use of the guiding metaphors discussed earlier. For example, the Heaven/Earth/Man system, where stones can represent all three elements or only some of them. The tallest rock in the garden on the facing page sits atop the mountain and transmits Heaven's energy into the Earth stones, the low boulders, and stone flooring. The midsize rocks (on either side of the fire) distribute the energy from above to below. They are the Man element.

In another system, of Earth/Water/Fire/Air/Space, stones can again be any of these five elements. The section of the garden on page 32 shows how these elements can come together in a balanced way. The Fire element here is both the actual fire of the tiki torches, as well as the trees. (As plants, these Bakeri spruces express the fire of the sun that gives them their vital energy.) The Water element is the waterfall and the river flowing under the bridge. Air is the movement on the path that is enticed through the narrow rock "gate" and out to the lawn and patio. Stone here, in the forms of the bridge, the patio, and the gateway rocks, is the Earth element of the garden. Space, the final element, is manifest in the spaciousness that arises when all the other four elements are present and balanced.

In the esoteric system, stones usually symbolize the Absolute, the realm of the ancients, the unchanging. It is ironic that stone, the most solid of garden-building materials, is symbolic of this most invisible realm.

Rock takes on this Absolute aspect when it is used correctly in the garden. The stones, as Absolute, must relate to the rest of the garden, where the Connection and the Manifest, each represented by other material elements, are also present.

The designer cannot use the metaphorical systems while ignoring the actual physical space and its spirit. Every garden is located in a region and climate, which heavily influence the choices made in type and composition of design. Mosko was born and raised in the Rocky Mountains and returned to them when he began to build gardens seriously. Therefore his usual style relies heavily on creating mountains and the use of evergreens in the planting plans. But he does not carry that into an inappropriate setting—he must respond to the environment where the garden will live. For example,

A section of a garden showing a balance of elements.

in Los Angeles his defining plants have been bamboo species. In a design for a lakeside house in New York the predominant feeling was placid and utilized primarily water elements.

Although using the metaphors will help to understand the direction of the design of rock arrangements and mountains, the metaphors will not finally tell you when harmony and balance have been achieved. The only way to be certain of that is to view the rock and mountain from the quiet mind arising from meditation. Remember that the outer mandala, which you create in part with rock, corresponds to an inner mandala of the body. In meditation, one becomes familiar with the stability of the mandala with a mind that is balanced, open, and clear. From this mind-set, looking at the arrangement and the harmony of the stones with the other parts of the garden becomes easier, and the judgment as to when everything is correct is more certain.

When balance is achieved, when the metaphors are fully realized, when the inner sanctity of the place can be felt by anyone entering the garden, when the stones are properly set—there is a sweet peace of place. Meditation and realization become natural as the soul arrives at its calm center.

Understanding

balance comes from a

meditative mind.

When all is in

harmony, a gentle

peace reigns.

Water

The form that water takes in a garden is often referred to as a "water feature," an unfortunate term that trivializes it by making water a commodity. Waterfalls, streams, ponds, and rivulets are not simply interchangeable components of a design; they create magic in the garden space. Where there is water, there is life: water gives birth to being.

Water has been used in gardens since the earliest civilizations. Canals bringing water from mountains to towns and fields inspired the first aesthetic use of water, and their rectilinear nature influenced the first shapes of water in gardens.[1] The Romans were famous for their ingenuity with water: in the ruins of Pompeii we can see how they made courtyard gardens complete with pools and fountains.[2] Islamic cultures used water in their gardens for both aesthetic and practical purposes. When Islam swept into Andalusia, the somewhat greater availability of water resulted in water becoming the dominant feature of the gardens.[3] The influence of these Moorish gardens extended into medieval Christian monasteries, where cloister gardens developed the theme of a walled paradise, often with water at the center.[4] The European garden tradition formalized the feel and shape of water, such as at Versailles near Paris and the Villa d'Este at Tivoli. The Oriental tradition tended to use water in a manner more imitative of nature.[5] Not until the romantic landscape tradition of

Water is given definition by rock,
or by its edges.

seventeenth and eighteenth century England did Western garden designers follow suit.

There must always be water in the garden, if only to water the plants. Water is part of the mandala of the garden, providing the animating energy of the space, even when it is represented by some other material. If it isn't possible to bring actual water into the landscape, a water basin or dry streambed will do; to complete the garden, water must be present in some way. Such water substitutes should suggest the movement or stillness of water.

Water is a unique element of the garden in that it has no fixed form itself. It is the only "contained" element, like the mind in the body. The qualities of water are much like the qualities of mind: still or dancing, silent or singing. And like the mind, water relates with the materials around it for its definition and shape.

Water has the qualities of clarity, purity, freshness, and power, and using it in the garden evokes those aspects. Not all of them are present at all times in all gardens, but by looking at each quality we can understand how the energy of water is expressed. Each inherent quality of water evokes an emotional response, which in turn informs the overall feel of the garden.

Water's clarity is expressed both through its depth and its power to reflect. Looking down through clean water is one way to understand the very idea of clarity. To look through the surface of water to the layers below

If the water is mind,

fish are like thoughts.

41

is to approximate the experience of looking deeply into
the mind, past the surface chatter of ordinary consciousness. In both cases we can see how the ripples of
daily activity do not change the qualities that lie under
the surface.

To maintain this experience, water can be kept clear
in various ways: through filtration, chemicals, or by creating a balanced ecosystem. Plants and fish can be used
to help create a system that is both self-cleaning and rea-
sonably self-sustaining. The plants restrict the amount of
light reaching the water, thereby controlling algae
growth. Some fish eat algae or insects, which maintains
the clarity of the water. (Interestingly, some Japanese
believe that koi fish were naughty monks in their last
lives. Some families have fish that have survived many
generations and are venerated for their longevity.)

The clarity of water is also demonstrated by the
opposite of clear depth: reflectivity. A large shallow
pool will double the image of all that is around it and
echo the color of the sky. A deep pool will glow with
subtle shifts of color. Reflection has a profound effect
on those gazing into it.

In the Japanese and other landscape traditions, the
purity of water is often literally employed to cleanse
the body and mind. This is epitomized by the *tsukubai* (a
bamboo spout which drops a stream of water into a
basin) used in teahouse garden design. The teahouse is a
place for the ultimate expression of Japanese culture,

during which both host and guest are committed to elegance of movement, beauty of speech, complete mindfulness, and sharing enlightened energy. The tsukubai is a means to cleanse oneself physically, mentally and spiritually, before entering the teahouse. Visitors rinse their mouths and splash water over their faces before entering the teahouse.

The third inherent quality of water is its kinesthetic quality of freshness: it can be cooling on a hot day, or it can warm you when the weather is cold. These kinesthetic qualities can be felt directly, by tasting the water from a tsukubai or stepping into a hot tub.

Another quality of water is its power. We can see the power of water in hurricanes and floods, and its power is evident even in its absence, in drought. Our ancestors harnessed the power of water to grind grain and cut wood and stone; today hydroelectric power is a major source of clean energy. In the garden, water's power is exercised in a latent form. Too much turbulence in the water would upset the peaceful atmosphere, so loud, ungoverned water designs should be avoided. Instead, the power of water may be suggested by carving a rock near the turning of a river to demonstrate how in time water can even wear down stone.

Apart from these inherent qualities, water can lend two aspects to the garden not readily available through other means: movement and sound. Movement of water in a garden is like the movement of energy in a

Water can warm you on a cold day.

Where there is water, there is life: water gives birth to being.

Facing page: The power of water is seen in a large waterfall.

mandala. Water allows the perception of movement, even in stillness. Movement can liberate the stream of thoughts, it can move our consciousness from one place to another. It makes us feel calm and extremely alive and aware.

Whether moving or still, water can lead us on a journey through the garden. It can do this either visually, by leading the eye, or physically, running along the side of a path. In either case the water pulls you into the experience of the garden. This use of water was pioneered in the Western world by the sixteenth-century Italian Bramante, who designed the Vatican's Cortile del Belvedere. He used water to give a sense of progression through the garden from one place to another.[6]

Water seeks a level place and so do people. This is why it is natural to put patios and other stopping places on level ground. The flow of water should be related to the movement of people through the garden. Paths and streams are linked. The two can play with and against each other, so that the path and the watercourse diverge and meet again in several places. The stone and the topography set the course of the stream, but the path has more freedom: one can lose the stream and then regain it, one can wander away from the stream into a flowery meadow, then return to sit by the water. Thoughtful garden design creates a dance in the movement of both water and people.

46   Water is also the main sound element of the garden. Though wind passing through the leaves of the plants can make sound, and birds and animals have their calls, these are not consistent. The only reliable sound is of water. Choosing the texture and shape of water depends upon the kind of music one wants to create. The garden creator must first have the desired feeling in mind, then imagine how that feeling is expressed in sound. Different music creates and enhances different kinds of moods. A waterfall leaves one energized with sound; streams can be active and vigorous, or slow and meandering; a pond can be still and reflective, or alive with fish and plants. Still another kind of music is silence. Everything relates to silence, and every garden should have silent places.

The inherent qualities of water, as well as its movement and sound, help to determine how water is used in a design. First, determine the feeling desired: is it innocent, compassionate, illuminating? If it is illuminating, the designer might create a very still bit of water, with a black bottom, so the reflection of all that is around it is extremely bright. One must ponder deeply to understand what form to use, and how to give expression to it through the use of the rock and plants around the water.

Water is often at the heart of the garden. Though Italian and French formal gardens often use the center of the space to place water and organize all other things

Water creates a symphony of sounds, from a quiet murmur to a crashing roar.

The heart-center is not necessarily the geographic center of the garden.

around it, the Japanese had a critical insight: that the geography of the mandala can be skewed. They moved the "center" off-center. This gives the mandala both a more subtle, hidden quality and a more discoverable and earthy relationship to people. It is tweaked to give it a less-than-perfect shape. The Japanese aesthetic relies on slight imperfection: just as the best tea bowl is the one with a small flaw, it is through imperfection the ultimate perfection is knowable.

Deciding what the heart of the garden is comes in part from clients, and often the water is the most important part of what they express. One client recalled the dream of a garden she had as a little girl. She remembered vividly the image and sound of water in the garden and could describe it, so that the vision she had remembered all her life could become a reality. Not all people can articulate their subconscious dreams as well as she did, but most of us have had them, and have a need to express them.

The heart-center is also defined by the movement of the sun and the moon and the cardinal directions, but also in part by the existing plants, which create patterns of light and shadow, and the shape of the land, which influences how the air and wind flow through the garden. Sometimes this heart-center is a long way from the physical center, but it is the place in the garden where the energy is most attuned and gathered. It is the radiant center of enlightened energy, and all else is

Water is not simply one possible component of the garden; it is the Connection between all the parts.

organized around it. It can be a mountain, but it is often a pond or other water.

Designing water in the garden can be made easier by referring again to the metaphors described in the first chapter. In the Heaven/Earth/Man metaphor, water can represent any of those elements, though because of the horizontal nature of water seeking a level state, it is most easily used as Earth. But water can also fall, taking a vertical form, which can represent Heaven. Water in a tall basin or in a fountain can also be representative of Man.

In the Earth/Water/Fire/Air/Space metaphor, Water is an essential member of the five elements. It must be present to lend balance and harmony to the design, though as previously mentioned its presence can be suggested through the use of raked gravel, dry riverbeds, and the like.

In any design, one difficulty that arises is that of balance. How does one assure that water doesn't overwhelm the garden; how does one know what size it should be? James van Sweden, a noted landscape designer, says about this balance:

> My travels in Japan reversed my opinion concerning the size of lily pools in a garden. It is not unusual for a lily pool in Japan to occupy one-third of the garden space. Now I am convinced it is important to err on the side of too large. My

first trip to Japan taught me that the bigger the pool, the better the garden.[7]

The key is to understand balance, but that is often a matter of personal taste. Some people err with more water, some err on the side of large rocks. The area that water can occupy is affected by the fact that water can represent other elements or metaphors as well. It can be space, it can be movement, so even a huge area of water can be balanced when it brings other elements into play.

In our most esoteric metaphorical system, Water is the element of Connection and compassion. The Connection is sometimes symbolized by images of powerful women, like the *dakinis* of Tibetan Buddhism. The Connection is the animating force, the force that brings life and active consciousness, which is fully alive. A single drop of water reflects all existence. It contains everything from the most minute to the vastest form. It is expressed as everything from the most gentle force (dew), to the most horrific (hurricanes and tidal waves). Water is that which connects the Absolute to the Manifest. It is the catalyst that creates the geometry of existence and brings it to life.

This can be seen in the waterfall: the rocks arrange the empty space, but only after water occupies it does the land suddenly burst into life. The water is the connection between the heavens and the earth as it flows from the

Terrace at Nyorai-an.

top of the fall under the influence of gravity. It is a physical connection in the flow, and an imaginative connection, when the sky above is reflected in the pond below.

Mosko trained with Japanese master gardeners in the use of water. The first was Katsushita Yamazaki, with whom he built three gardens, including the courtyard at the Boulder Public Library and another in east Boulder. This was the first time Mosko watched a Japanese waterfall being built. Since the space was small, the first thing they did was to build a wall around it, and at one end piled dirt against one side of it to create a mountain. (This technique is used frequently in Japan, where if there's no room for a complete mountain, a wall is built, and just the front side of the mountain is constructed against it.) From the mountain, they created a waterfall about six inches wide. At the end, the water spills into a natural fall and then a bamboo funnel. This little garden encapsulates the relationship between the mountain and the water. Everything relates to a mountain, even if the mountain isn't physically present in the garden. Even a pond in a meadow relates to a mountain theme, because the meadow implies the mountain.

With a second Japanese master gardener, Yoshinori Murakami, Mosko built the garden *Nyorai-an.* The slope in this garden is about three to one and it is carved into three distinct terraces, forming mountains and bringing water across and down each level.

53

The pond at the second level of Nyorai-an.

The garden starts with a small rivulet running through a narrow channel over small shards of rock, which makes a bright sound; then that turns into a small, quiet stream twelve to eighteen inches wide, which meanders down the hill. The entrance of the water is at the top, and it runs in a series of cascades down the levels. The fall from the first to the second level occurs in front of the teahouse on the second level, which is cantilevered out over the pond created at the bottom of the fall. Thus the teahouse looks at created scenery, the river and the rocks. In digging the three levels, Murakami Sensei also created the relationship among the rocks at each level, which in turn directed the flow of the water.

In building *Nyorai-an,* Mosko learned the intimate relationship between how the rocks are set and how the water exists in the garden. In Japanese gardens there are almost always a few rocks at the edges. The rocks are reflected in the water, creating a beautiful effect. *Nyorai-an* demonstrates the music of water and how to use the pathway in conjunction with the water, as ways to create dreamy pictures.

After all his training and later experience, Mosko Sensei has developed his own methods of working with water in design and construction. As he designs, he keeps in mind both the qualities of water (purity, clarity, freshness, and power), as well as the senses of movement and sound it will create. Most importantly,

To look through the surface of water to the layers below is to approximate the experience of looking deeply into the mind, past the surface chatter of ordinary consciousness.

Below: First you think of what kind of heart is expressed by the water.

Facing page: "After" view (looking south) at Blessings Come Down, *showing both patios. Left: "Before" view of the same area.*

he believes, in a garden, the idea of compassion and connection is expressed in water, and this is frequently the most important aspect of what the garden is.

In the garden *Blessings Come Down,* for example, the water expresses the love and connection in the family which owns it. The owners moved to the city from the mountains for business reasons, and missed the beauty of the natural landscape. The distance from the back door to the street was small and steep, with a view included a smokestack and a school as well as imposing mountain forms known locally as the Flatirons.

Thinking about how to design this garden during a visit to the mountains, Mosko realized that the closer you are to a mountain, the more majestic it appears. This inspiration informed the entire design: he re-created a mountain very close to the back door, with the water running from top to bottom, like the blessings of the family members' love for each other.

The original patio space was cramped. To change the feeling of the area, the mountain and the water are pushed right up to the door, leaving room only for a few steps down from the back door. The patio areas bulge out to the north and south of the door, seeming more spacious for being broken into two. The north patio area offers a view of the mountains, and the arching fence also serves to block the nearby buildings and road. The rocks on the right deliberately echo the Flatirons, bringing the larger scene into the garden. The

Left: "After" view (looking north) at Blessings Come Down, showing two of the falls. Below: "Before" view of the same area.

A long time ago,

before language, we

came upon a pond,

and for the first time

saw our own image.

This is an extremely

powerful experience,

one that is repeated

in every pool.

south patio area looks up the stream, with water coming down toward the viewer. From the inside of the house, the upper pond reflects rocks behind and emphasizes the presence of the mountain. Rocks here are the Heaven/Earth/Man arrangement, and the water is the base for the rocks and the connection to them.

Again, in order to see when the correct proportions and balances have been achieved, the designer must look with eyes conditioned by meditation. Creating the right feel of water is a contemplative experience arising from a certain state of mind, not something arbitrary or something achieved by application of standard rules. The relationship with water should be personal and intimate. On both on a practical and metaphorical level, in the West we have relegated water to a diminished role. We should instead offer water the respect and understanding that it deserves. When we create a waterfall, a stream, or pond, think of it as expressing enlightenment, and always try to convey that energy. The water is not simply one possible physical part of the garden; it is the connection between all the parts.

Fire

The Fire element of the garden is represented by its plants, the expression of the heat and light of the sun. Fire is passion and excitement, but it is also comfort and help—for cooking food or boiling water—and it is light. People are beings of light; we need light to feed ourselves and to remain sane. Plants use light as a critical part of photosynthesis. They literally are light, and they nourish lightness and warmth in people. This is one reason why we make connections between plants and emotional events: the red roses to a lover on Valentine's Day; the white lilies at a grave; the cheer of a bouquet to ease the atmosphere of a hospital room.

Plants rely upon the earth for support and structure, and on water for nutrients. Plants balance with earth and water to give the garden its character. These three elements form a triangle, a balance of three. Of course, plants are not the only life of the garden. They are the living element of the garden but they result from the balance and contribution of the other elements. It's as though when you add the Fire (plants) to the Earth and Water, life suddenly springs forth, like a match added to tinder creates a leap of flames.

Plants lead the spiritual mind into greater depths of understanding. The prophet of Islam, Muhammad, climbed an olive tree in his dreams and was overcome by the beauty revealed to him at the top. The Tree of Knowledge and the Garden of Eden are central to the Book of Genesis.[1] The Buddha gained enlightenment

Facing page: Dogen called the nature of reality "flowers in space."

Left: Flowers are the richness of the mandala.

while sitting under the bo tree. Seeing the interdependent nature of plants with the other elements leads to a clearer understanding of the phrase used by Dogen, the founder of Japanese Zen. He called the nature of reality "flowers in space."

A gardener must start with this understanding of plants as the fire of the sun, as both heat and light. Light may appear as clear, but when refracted shows itself to be a spectrum of color. This is the basis for designing color in the garden. Color theory, though useful in plant design, is misguided when it becomes formulaic. If we compose flowers by formula or system, we occlude the natural expression of the space. Garden magic arises when plant design flows from a contemplative rather than a formulaic mind.

Flowers are the richness of the mandala, changing its focus and lending each area of it its own particular qualities. Each color has an energy in itself and in combination and contrast to the others. The power of the color can partly be internal and partly external in its comparison, compatibility, and contrast with other colors and shapes.

One means of understanding color is as the expression of different kinds of energy. For example, many Buddhists describe five basic kinds of energy, each of which is associated with a color.[2] There is a clear, cool energy of wisdom that sees things as they are, which is associated with blue. There is an energy of richness,

fulfillment, and fruition, which is yellow. There is an energy of passion and seduction, which is red. The energy of activity and accomplishment is green. And there is an energy of calm knowing, of peaceful understanding, associated with white.[3]

Color is not something designed into the garden in the absence of any other consideration. "You also need to think about the shapes and textures of flowers and foliage because it is surprising how much these influence our experience of color," says one noted plant designer.[4]

Not only the texture of the plants and their shapes affect our experience of color, but the color interacts with other colors, with the structures and pathways of the garden, and with the energy of the rocks and water and space that surround the colors chosen. The plants are part of an energetic pattern, as are the rest of the elements of the garden; they don't stand alone. "Plant design" can't be a separate part of the garden design, since it must work with the existing energy of the garden as well as the remainder of the mandala. It is integral to the design process, not simply an added layer or decorative overlay.

In deciding how to arrange the plants in the garden, the three metaphorical systems we've discussed can be useful.

In the Heaven/Earth/Man metaphor, which describes the physical relationship of the elements,

The designer must keep in mind the mature height of the plants to maintain their correct relationships.

plants can represent any of the elements. Trees can represent Heaven as they are higher than other plants, and overhead. The Man element is the intermediate size, from three to seven feet in height, which we can relate to because it is the same general size and scope of the human form. Shrubs are generally used as the Man element. Flowers are often used as the Earth element. Since this metaphor describes the physical relationship among the elements of the garden, the designer must always keep in mind the full mature height of each plant in order to create the right relationships.

Plants are the Fire element in the five-element metaphorical system, because they are related to the sun's heat and light. The spectrum of color is an expression of light. If plants themselves are not present, they must be implied, just as the element of Water can be suggested by a dry riverbed of cobble. All the elements of the garden mandala are necessary to create a balanced space. Even the most austere Japanese gardens almost always have lichen on the rocks, or a small number of plants. Raked sand and rock arrangements may be works of art, in the way that sculptures are works of art, but they are not gardens in the sense that we are describing here.

In the three realms metaphor, Absolute/Connection/Manifest, plants are form, the Manifest. Plants are impermanent by their nature, as is the Manifest. We see leaves flutter in the breeze, we see

Impermanence is the hallmark
of the Manifest.

them change color in the seasons, we see flowers bloom and wither. This impermanence is the hallmark of the Manifest.

Trees are unusual among plants in that they can represent a variety of elements within each metaphorical system. They can be tall enough to be Heaven, or medium-sized to be Man. As plants they are expressions of the Manifest, but since they reach deeply into the earth and upward toward the heavens, they can also represent the Connection between the Absolute and the Manifest. In fact, the Japanese especially like to see the roots of the trees, since they are a fuller expression of how Heaven is brought down into the Earth. The roots gather water and mix it with the Earth, while the branches reach toward the sky—the tree becomes a full demonstration of the unity of elements that create life.

There are other principles beyond the metaphors that assist in plant design. For example, there must be variation in sizes so that any given size can be appreciated. A garden of all tall trees would actually reduce the sense of size that such trees could otherwise provide. Plant design is like the use of dynamics in music: a loud tone is emphasized by the subdued sound of those around it. Also, within each element there should be harmony in the relationships; for example, a harmony of trees among trees and flowers among flowers. Third, one of the principles of Japanese gardening is

Facing page: Trees express the unity of the elements.

Left: There are moments in meditation and in the garden when time vanishes.

that a garden should derive from a specific sense of place, and be completely at home in its surroundings. Plants are fundamental to the integration of the garden with its larger world, so the contemplative garden should have native, or at least appropriate, plants, no matter what style the garden uses.

Another aspect of plants is important to keep in mind as part of the design: plants provide the sense of time in the garden. Though water flows and rocks erode, these parts of the passage of time seem invisible to us as we observe the garden. But the birth, growth, and decay of the plants in the garden are obvious. It is the life cycle of the plants that gives a window into the flow of time in the garden.

Through sensing how time passes, we can also sense the unceasing nature of life. A particular plant will grow, wither, and die, but plants themselves are the restless energy of light—there will always be another coming to take the place of those that have passed on. A single plant is limited in time; the thrust of life is timeless and ongoing.

Plants offer the element of time to the garden. But does a mandala exist in time, or is it timeless? Both the inner mandala (of the body) and outer mandala (expressed in the garden) have "relative" and "ultimate" aspects. The ultimate does not exist in time; it is independent of time. The relative mandala exists in time

The green garden is the place of activity.

and space. In meditation, we can see how both relative and ultimate are different aspects of the same thing.

It is possible to step into the perception of the unity of the absolute and relative when everything is in balance within your mind and in the environment. There are moments in meditation when time vanishes, and the meditator goes beyond conscious thought to sense the integration and oneness of all that exists. At these moments, we can see clearly the indivisibility of the absolute and the relative realms. When our balance is upset, when the natural entropy of cellular and mental life intrudes, we experience the delusion of a separation between the absolute and relative.

Upon arising from meditation, we can carry with us the remembrance that the two realms, ultimate and relative, are the same. We may only experience their unity in moments of great calm, and great quiet. But by creating a contemplative garden, and being in it, we work with elements that change as part of their fundamental natures (as plants do) to rediscover and manifest that which is beyond time and space. We contact the ultimate by focusing on the impermanence of existence. The flower that blooms and dies in the same day gives that sense of uniqueness and preciousness of every moment in the life of the flower. In that, we encounter timelessness.

White is the color of purity.

An example of a garden which brings all these principles together is called *Flowers in Space,* after Dogen's description of reality. (This garden is more fully explored in the Fruition section.) This garden is a complete world encompassing all the energies of the universe organized within a mandala. The colors of the plants work with the topography of the land to bring each section of the garden into harmony. There are three valleys and nine mountains, each with its own meaning and emotion. These meanings and emotions are exemplified and intensified by the plant colors used in each section. The blue garden is cool and clear, and provides the best view of all the other areas. The yellow garden is in a valley, lush with plants and ripeness. The white garden is calm and inviting, with a low mountain covered in white blossoms, and with a flat reflecting pool. The red garden is passionate with red flowers and hidden spaces for lovers. The green garden is for the activities of the family, with room for games and picnics under the trees. Towering over it all is Mount Sumeru, the embodiment of the center of the universe, with a cave buried at its heart. Mount Sumeru is covered with 1,500 alpine plants of all sizes and colors. While moving from one part of the garden to another, the color changes enhance the sense of time passing. This landscape is a triumph of plant design precisely because the plants are an integral part of the design, balanced with

Facing page: Yellow stands for richness and fulfillment.

Left: Blue is the color of clarity and wisdom.

the rocks and water, not some later addition that was not part of the original vision.

Plants in the garden delight the eye with their colors, the nose with the luxury of scent. They enable the garden to engage and occupy the senses, and when the senses are occupied, no thoughts arise. The meditative mind has created a contemplative space, which in turn induces the meditative mind in all who enter. Breathe out, and the garden has become part of you; breathe in, and you are part of the garden.

Left: The red garden has hidden places
for lovers.

Below: The meditative mind creates a contemplative
space, which in turn induces the meditative mind.

Air

The garden can be restful but it is never still. Water runs or shimmers in the sun; plants grow and die; the wind rustles the leaves of the trees. And under these superficial levels of activity, the "air" of the garden flows. What we call here the Air element is an expression of the energy of the garden itself. Though air is invisible, the manifest forms of air are the paths and structures of the garden.

Air energy, though unseen, is an integral part of the landscape. Since ancient times people have been aware of the energy of the earth. The Druids used it to guide the placement of their stone circles; the Aboriginal people follow their invisible "songlines"; and the Chinese developed the art of geomancy they now call *feng shui*. This system is based on the earth's own energy, called *chi* (also spelled *qi*) by the Chinese. Feng shui is a conglomeration of three related ideas: the principle of the opposites (yin and yang), the principle of constant change, and the five elements that the Chinese believe make up all the phenomena of the visible world.[1] Feng shui is the art of discovering the harmony between opposites and the elements in an ever-changing environment. It was imported from China to Japan (where it is called *fusui*) in the eighth century and gradually became the basis for instructions on building gardens and homes in accord with the energy of the land they occupied.[2]

We can recognize the many ways in which the earth has energy simply by thinking of the magnetic poles, the

The human body is an energy system.
Photo © Thomas Laird. From The Dalai Lama's
Secret Temple: Tantric Wall Paintings from Tibet
by Ian A Baker, published by Thames & Hudson,
London and New York.

absorption of sunlight, the pull of gravity, or the molten core of the earth that occasionally erupts to the surface in volcanoes. We know that the earth's crust moves constantly, releasing energy in earthquakes. There is no question that the earth contains energy, though in the West we have not sought to measure or systematize it in the same way or in the same terms that the Chinese have.

We seek to harmonize our man-made landscapes with the energy of the earth because the earth's energy in turn affects us. We are, after all, also an energy system. As noted physician Dr. Andrew Weil suggests, if we use the physics definition of energy as the ability to do work, it is obvious that body processes like the beating heart, digestion, and hormone manufacture are all energy phenomena.[3] Chinese medicine is based on an understanding of the body's energy, again called chi, the same term for the energy of the earth. In Chinese medicine, the body is viewed as being made up of a balance of yin and yang as well as the five elements, and as constantly changing, just like the earth. Energy flows throughout the body along recognized lines called meridians, which are accessible to change through acupuncture. Hindu and Buddhist systems of thought also include the view that an unseen energy called in Sanskrit *prana* flows through the body along *nadis* (channels). This energy gathers and pools in vortices called *chakras* (nodes).

Going up or down, or using unevenly spaced stepping-stones, can make people slow down on the path.

What is this thing called prana or chi that runs through both the land and our bodies? One Daoist priest translates the chi ideogram as "formless fire of life."[4] Chi is life, but it has no physical substance and is not measurable. And how is it that it can be the same thing in both earth and living body? This is not a contradiction. Physicists tell us that "The distinction between organic and inorganic is a conceptual prejudice . . . The philosophical implication of quantum mechanics is that all of the things in our universe (including us) that appear to exist independently are actually parts of one all-encompassing organic pattern, and that no parts of that pattern are ever really separate from it or from each other."[5] Thus, both modern physics and ancient wisdom lead us to conclude that the connections between the earth and ourselves are real.

In a contemplative garden, the inner mandala of the self and the outer mandala of the garden utilize this energetic connection. The quiet mind of meditation is reflected in the peaceful space of the garden because they are both the same kind of energy.

That energy, or chi, or prana, is the Air element, and it is brought into form in the paths and structures of the garden. Paths should lead us through the garden along lines that reflect the energy of the earth. It is through the pathway, and the structures that occur along the path, that man is invited to join with nature and experience its energy.

Facing page: Curving paths are feminine forms that undulate and turn.

Right: Bridges represent going from one state of mind to another.

The understanding of the energy of the garden arises with the vision of the garden, as some kind of poetry. Once you understand the character of the garden you are designing, it becomes easier to design the paths that flow through it. They are simply the connections that bring the vision of the garden to life.

Paths are like the notes on a sheet of music, which define movement and dynamics but are not themselves music. When you hear music, it is different from looking at the notes printed on the page. In the same way, the path only gives the opportunity to experience the garden. What you actually experience is affected by your consciousness and your physical abilities. A taller viewer might see over a wall or hedge, for example. A more distracted visitor might not see the tiny arrangement of pebbles and low flowers at his feet, where a visitor with a quiet mind might take it in. Just as everyone who hears a piece of music will get something different out of it, so everyone will have a different experience of the garden.

The garden path is slow because contemplative or meditative walking is always slow. In Soto Zen, there is a half step taken with each breath in walking meditation. (In some schools the pace is faster—in the winter, practitioners run around the outside of the meditation hall!) When the pace is slow, there's no separation from meditation mind, there's no rush, and the mind can be calm.

To encourage people to slow down, make the experience along the path so compelling that one does

not want to rush by. The path can narrow or become rougher, with stepping-stones, for example, to slow down the pace. Set stones as a walkway across water, which is quite safe but requires concentration to negotiate. The path can go up or down, which also brings the mind to a sharper awareness. Steps make people slow down, particularly if they are uneven in height or spacing. Crossing a bridge or other threshold also slows people down.

Views unfold along paths. A common pond shape in Japanese gardens, for example, is roughly in the shape of the character for "heart." There are few places along the shore where the entire pond's edge can be seen, because of the way that land intrudes. Thus with each step along the path, hidden views are revealed, and other views hidden. This "concealing and revealing" technique is one way to make small spaces seem larger, since there are always new views to see. Going up and down along topography does the same thing, since it generally forces you to look down for most of the time. Then when you reach the top or the bottom, a view can spread out before you as a little surprise. The gaze, which has been down, is suddenly open to something elementally beautiful, like sunlight on a rose.

Bridges are special aspects of paths. If water represents mind, the bridge represents crossing from one state to another. In that awareness of change, we become fresh and new. The designer can use a bridge

Facing page: The gaze can suddenly be met with something beautiful, like sunlight on roses.

Right: The fence can be solid or transparent, depending on how much of the surrounding landscape you wish to enter the garden.

even over a dry riverbed or other landscape feature that is not water to create this sense of movement to a different state of mind, or as a transition to a new view. It is especially good to use a bridge as part of an entry path to the house, since the bridge is symbolic of moving from the outer world to the inner.

All gardens must have an enclosure, or skin, for their energetic systems. There have to be boundaries in order to have a balanced composition. In the same way that paintings are limited to a canvas, the garden has to have a limit which establishes the "frame" of the composition. As in painting, the boundaries themselves establish certain laws of composition within their domain. The first stroke of a calligraphy creates a rhythm, a relation between the ink and the edge that is indelible. In the same way, the boundary relates to the first stone set, and that relationship influences the organization that follows.

Even in a very large space, any focal point area will have to have some sense of boundary. The boundary can be naturally existing, such as a ridgeline or a natural depression in the land, or it can be man-made, like property lines and fences. A fence can be made in any style, but since it defines the space, thinking about it at the beginning is critical.

As much as possible it is good to have a soft boundary. Fencing isn't soft but it is precise. Fences can be more or less noticeable: a wall or a thicket of shrubs.

The structure is located where the river makes a sharp turn, and opposite it is a mountain of flowers.

They can be solid or transparent, depending on how much of the surrounding landscape's view and energy you want to have enter the garden, and at what point. The height is also important, for purposes of screening or revealing different parts of the surroundings. The fence plays a role in bringing the macrocosm (the larger landscape) into the microcosm (the garden) by allowing only certain views of the macrocosm.

The nature of the boundary will influence the feeling of the garden. For example, there are communities where the backyards meet one another, and only low fences are permitted. This can foster the sense of community. Other places allow high walls, which create a more internal experience, and make the garden enclosed by them more of a refuge.

Fences can be used to separate one part of a garden from another. In a composition made up of distinct areas such as patios and pools, or entertainment areas and contemplation areas, it may be a good idea to separate one area from another visually or physically with a fence. The means of getting from one area to another then becomes very important for setting the stage for the next experience of the garden. The style of the gate of the fence, its dimensions, and its color, are all important in preparing someone for what is to come.

In every instance, the entrance to a garden is an important consideration. It sets the first impression and makes the introduction to the space and its poetry. In

Chinese gardens, one first enters a small outdoor "room," then passes through another gateway into the first taste of the garden proper. The entrance should help to make the walker aware of entering a special space.

Any entrance can be controlled by establishing a threshold, such as a bridge over water, a gateway of some sort, or plants such as an allée of trees or an opening in a hedge. Whatever is used should mark a break from what went before. Entrances are the first means of controlling the pace of the people entering. Slowing down the mind allows the recognition of entering a different space. The entrance establishes the mind and the mood.

Having the entrance and the exit the same gives the most control. Some gardens place the house at the center of the garden: then, you control the number of accesses to the garden by controlling the number of ways to access it from the house. A garden can have multiple entrances and exits, but in a garden mandala, there should be a maximum of four; more than that and there's no control of access and views. Most of the time the path circulates through the garden and returns to its origin. In some way the path either leads to or acknowledges all four directions.

There are gardens that are meant to be viewed from some remote vantage, not walked through, and these have no paths. They are like three-dimensional paintings, and need only hidden access for maintenance. At the same time, they still have an energetic system. The energy has to be implied with something other than paths, perhaps with the rise and fall of topography, or a dry riverbed.

A structure affords a way to get off the path. It can be a widening of the path (with different material underfoot, for example), a stone that you can stand or sit on, or an elaborate, enclosed structure. Often, the architect of a home tries to blend any structure in the garden with the house, while the garden designer tries to blend it with the garden. The important thing to remember is that since it is rare that both structures are seen simultaneously, they need not match in any formal way. However, both the home and the garden structure are part of the same energetic system, the mandala, and thus must be harmonious. Both architect and landscape architect must work together to ensure that this harmony is achieved.

The structure is part of the picture of the garden that arises in conjunction with the energy of the whole. Paths are a means for consciousness to move through the space, and structures complete that purpose by offering points to stop and consider the landscape in peace. When you make a place that's protected and comfortable, where people can relax and ease their minds, then they can experience the garden and view with the right mind.

Structures are located along paths in places where energy gathers, usually where a major view appears. When you compose a garden, you must do so from some

Some structures are tranquil and inviting, places to drink tea and contemplate.

established vantage points, such as the windows of the house that overlook the garden, or from the doors and patios that lead out from the house, or from an entrance gate separate from the house. In every case, any structure you build in the garden must be visually pleasing from these vantage points. The structure must also have its own view from within toward the rest of the garden.

A structure might also be placed where one enters the heart-center of the garden, which is often water. An example is in the *Garden of the Healing Stones* (see pp. 90–91), where the structure is in the center of the garden. It is located where the stream makes a sharp turn, and opposite it is a mountain of flowers. It is a place for a nice view.

The style of the structure is dictated by the space, but it also imparts its own character to the garden. Grottoes and caves have almost no views, but these structures offer a profound experience of quiet and the internal. Entering them is like entering the energy of the womb. The grotto is an opportunity to do wonderful and imaginative things with grade, approach, and light. Above ground structures fall into two categories. The first is the structure that blends with the environment, is more modest and earthier. Many of Mosko's teahouses are of this type: tranquil and inviting, often with low ceilings, places to drink tea and to contemplate quietly.

The second type of structure falls under the rubric of a shrine. These are not cozy and protected; they are

The straight path is the path of wisdom.

*The structure can be an open place
to experience the divine.*

places to feel divine energy. Being in them brings a sense of elevation and recognition of the Absolute, of things larger than ourselves. These structures stand out, and are generally taller than anything surrounding them.

Both paths and structures can express masculine and feminine energies, and masculine and feminine emotional qualities. Masculine elements are straight, linear, geometrically angled, bold, upright, strong, and have a tendency toward dominance. Strength is the muscular, military kind of strength. Feminine elements are rounded, twisted, hidden, soft in texture and color, indefinite, and inviting. They are powerful in a more subtle way, like water that wears away stone.

According to Eva Wong, a well-respected feng shui master who lives in Colorado, straight, masculine paths are paths of wisdom, like those presented at a temple or church. The visitor goes fast and straight to the entrance and the source of truth. The path leads directly there.

Curving paths are paths of compassion, expressing constant unfolding and giving away of the heart. Almost always in the residential setting, Mosko uses the circuitous path. As people pass through the garden into the home, they should feel the spirit of compassion and beauty. Curving paths are feminine forms that undulate and turn, movement that looks like a woman's thigh. These are preferable when the architecture is masculine, with straight angles, hard lines, reflective glass, and hard materials. The garden has to offer feminine energy to balance and harmonize with that kind of building.

Paths and structures don't relate to the other elements of the garden in the same way that the other elements relate to each other. The paths can't be organized by the Heaven/Earth/Man metaphor, which describes physical relationships of the elements to one another, because fundamentally paths are an expression of energy. They are means to enter, stop, and leave the garden, not things that relate to the physical bodies of the garden. The structure itself may have ceiling, walls, and floor (Heaven/Earth/Man), but it doesn't relate to the other elements in this physical way because it is an extension of the energy of the pathway. Therefore they must exist in balance with all the other elements for the garden to feel complete.

Paths and structures are, however, part of the metaphor of Earth/Water/Fire/Air/Space. They represent the Air energy in this system, the movement and flow of energy through the garden and its gathering at certain crucial points.

Paths and structures are the Connection part of the metaphor of Absolute/Connection/Manifest. Just as air touches the earth and carries its fragrance to all the parts of the garden, so paths are the connection between the Absolute and the Manifest, touching both aspects of existence and bringing them together. Paths and structures represent something that is unseen but clearly felt.

Paths exemplify

Connection.

Space

Most of what we perceive as matter is made up of space. Even the building blocks of matter—molecules, atoms, and the subatomic particles that comprise them—contain space. If there were no space, atoms would collapse in upon themselves. There could be no form without the space that separates.

Our galaxy and the universe it is part of are mostly space, and some theories hold that matter as we know it is expanding further into space. The science of astrophysics confirms that we exist in some inconceivable vastness that has no boundary.

Space is the opposite of form and the antithesis of energy, so how is it present in the garden? One way in which space exists in the garden is as the volume between all the forms. This is similar to the "negative space" that painters, sculptors, and architects know and work with. It is the balancing element, without which we cannot understand the form itself. As the architect I. M. Pei said, "What else is there in architecture when you talk about form and space? It is the play between the solids and the voids."[1] Space is important in understanding composition in all art, since it is the background against which everything is seen, the vessel in which everything takes place.

Traditional Eastern and Western views of space differed widely. Where Western artists viewed space as a dead area that needed to be filled, artists of the Orient saw space as alive and organic, able itself to create a tension with other forms. Empty spaces in traditional

Facing page: It can be especially effective to provide views into enclosed, shady areas.

Right: Changing lines and patterns or breaking them up can open space in a way that delights the eye.

Chinese scroll paintings, for example, force the viewer to make imaginative leaps in order to understand the invisible connections between the forms on the paper.[2] Space can be used this way in the garden. Breaking lines of flowers in unexpected ways, building multiple arch-ways, moving from softscape to hardscape, changing lines and patterns or breaking them up can all open space in a way that both delights the eye and invites the viewer to participate in the creation of the garden.

Different areas of the garden might have different feelings of space. Coming into a small, protected area might encourage one to stop and sit. It can be especial-ly effective to provide views into enclosed, shaded areas from a more open area, since this kind of contrast offers an opportunity to climb out of a rut in the mind.

Using open areas above or beyond the garden perimeter is a way of connecting the smaller landscape with the larger, and making an area feel bigger. Space, after all, is infinite. A good garden design should be soaked in the sense of space so that the mind of the visi-tor is soaked in infinity.

This is the secret of designing a small garden. When the infinite can be glimpsed, when the presence of infinite space can be felt, the garden design has suc-ceeded. Since this also invites the character of the envi-ronment into the garden, it must be done carefully and selectively. The view need not even be long; it should only be open.

Neither we nor the garden can exist without light.

Space, however, is more than just this creative tension of solid and void. Just as the energy of the garden, though invisible, is reflected in the pathways and structures of the garden, so the Space element is understood by seeing how light moves in the garden. Whereas the heat and energy of light are expressed in the Fire element as plants, the aspect of light referred to here is its visual quality of illumination: it is the luminosity of the enlightened mind.

Light is a phenomenon existing simultaneously as a wave and a particle.[3] Attempts to understand light led to the development of quantum physics, and to this day scientists do not fully understand its qualities or behavior. But it is clear that neither we nor the garden can exist without light.

The way that light falls and moves in a garden is determined by the interplay of the solid forms and the spaces around them. I. M. Pei again: "Without the play of light, form is inert and space becomes static."[4] Light is a necessary part of our visual perception of the garden, and it is also crucial to our understanding of how its space works. James Turrell, an artist who has abandoned objects altogether in favor of creating shapes of light, explains that although light is intangible, it is physically felt. "My works are not a looking at, but a looking into; not the displacement of space with mass, but the working of space; not objects in a room, but the room. The format is not things within space, but space

itself."[5] This view is in accord with the scientific understanding we have that most of what we see as matter is really space. This is how the garden designer should envision the Space element, as something that co-exists with the other elements used in the garden, not something separate. Hard as it may be to understand, the space and the form exist at the same time.

Playing with light as an exemplar of space is an important part of garden design. As we move through a garden, both the feeling of the space and the quality of light change. Thus the garden's defining feeling is determined by the fluctuation, modulation, and flow of space, and the effect of the light.

There is a structure to the movement through the garden space. It consists of: contrasts of light and dark (what painters call chiaroscuro); the flow of space (the way one moves through volume); and the quality of light.

Using contrasts of light and dark is one way to organize space. Anything in shadow will retreat to the background of a view, and appear smaller. Lighter elements—brighter colored flowers, unshaded lawns— can help to frame and give order to the composition of the garden.

Trees and structures are the main source of shadow, and all other contrasts in light and color are viewed through the filter of light they create. If an entire area is covered with trees, the light may be too uniform and the space uninteresting. The shadow cast by the home

Facing page: The shadow cast by the home itself should be a design consideration.

Left: The effect of a red flower can be doubled in direct sun.

itself should be a consideration in design. Moving some garden element into this shadow can make it appear more dramatic in contrast to the elements in the sun beyond. These Heaven elements of trees and structures should be balanced carefully with Man and Earth elements to maintain the play of light and dark.

Shadow and light techniques are used in more than one dimension in the garden. They also have to do with an understanding of volumes as we move through space. For example, one might emerge from a shaded forest of trees onto the top of a rise that overlooks a sunny meadow. A path might be designed to run through a less interesting area in the shade, leading to a central attraction in the sun. This will draw viewers forward into the place you'd like them to be. A path beside a river could be placed in the sun or shade to change the impact of the view of the water and its surroundings. This is the control over the flow of space using light, making one area darker and another lighter to direct the flow of movement.

Finally, the quality of light can vary widely. It can be cool shade or moonlight, it can be dewy soft, or it can be brilliant and stimulating. The experience of garden space is dramatically affected by the sky, whether it is cloudy, rainy, or sunny, and by the shade cast by the various forms used.

The amount of light will affect how each color or the garden is perceived as well. The effect of a red

The experience of the garden is dramatically affected by the sky.

flower can be doubled if it is seen in direct sun. The water of a river will be reflective in bright light and more transparent in the shade, so that you can see the fish or the rocks on the bottom. Each quality of light imparts a different mood and a different sense of place.

This feeling will change throughout the day as the sun moves, revealing new aspects of shaded areas and concealing others. Even the same area will take on an entirely different look in the evening from its appearance at midday.

The change of seasons also brings a change in light. A landscape will look transformed in the cold, clear light of winter midday, when the sun is at a lower angle in the sky and there is less shade from trees without their leaves.

A designer should spend time on a site over the course of time, and at different times of day, to get an idea of how the trees and house already present affect the amount of sunlight available throughout. If it is not possible to see the site in all seasons, the owners may have photographs that can help. Good design combines these uses of light to compose a space and the movement through it.

By composing the flow of space and light, the garden designer strongly influences the visitor's perception and experience of time. A garden can be enlivening and breathtaking, or it can be calm and quiet: the mood and feeling of the garden are set through the control of

*The change of seasons
also brings a change of light.*

space. Time can be accelerated or slowed down by changing the degree to which the senses are engaged. If there is a lot happening, time seems to slow down as the mind tries to assimilate views and scents. Conversely, a clear, open, abstract composition will draw the mind in a different direction, so that once again the experience of time passing is different. This is similar to the control of dynamics in music. Loud sound has meaning in direct relation to the degree of softness played. What is important is not whether time is experienced as slow or fast, only that there are variations to entice the viewer out of the ordinary sense of time passing.

Space relates to the other elements of the garden, but not in a way characterized by the Heaven/ Earth/Man metaphor. It is intangible, without form, so it is not part of the physical relationship among forms described by this metaphor.

Space is one of the five elements of the Earth/ Water/Fire/Air/Space metaphor. As mentioned in the Earth chapter, Space arises correctly when the other elements are all present and balanced. We know when Space is correct using the same sense that tells us when a composition is right, either in two dimensions like a painting, or in three, as in the garden. This sense is our inner balance expressed in the outer world. Since everyone has their own degree of inner clarity, what is pleasing to one person will not always suit others.

The relationship of Space to Air (or energy) is different from its relationship to the other, material elements. Space and Air are more intimately tied together, almost two aspects of one thing. Space is a pull, an opening, a vastness that draws you in; Air, energy, is push, activity that expands outward. This tension and connection are visible in a garden when a path leads toward a stopping place, whether that is an open, sunny area or an enclosed and shaded place.

The balance of the elements should arise in conjunction with the vision of the garden. Garden designers must gather as much information as possible about the wishes of clients (including their unspoken desires), the climate, the soils, the spirit of the site, the way the light falls on the garden, and any other relevant considerations. This information must be allowed to ripen, without conscious thought, until the seed of understanding sprouts. From that seed will grow a vision of the entire garden, allowing one to know how it feels to be in the garden, the appropriate mood to create, and how the elements should be balanced.

The process of creating a garden is not to seek an elegant solution to "problems" on the site, or to adorn the architecture, or to devise a clever concept or theme. Instead, the guide is this pre-concept, pre-style vision about what the garden will feel like. This original clarity will dictate how the garden looks, how its elements interact, and other choices throughout the design process.

Facing page: The balance of the elements arises in conjunction with the vision of the garden.

Right: Time can be accelerated or slowed by changing the degree to which the senses are engaged.

Space can also be understood as part of the metaphor of the Absolute/Connection/Manifest. In this system, Space is part of the Absolute, the ultimate form of reality. It is neither alive nor not alive. The mandala of the garden arises out of space, and dissolves back into space. Space is the container for the garden, the background against which it takes form, but it is also a part of every atom of every form in the garden.

The metaphors help to understand how to make a coherent design. Understanding the physical, energetic, and metaphysical relationships among the elements helps to guide the process and to check on the success of the final product. But the true contemplative garden is an expression of the meditative mind, and only from that mind can one understand when balance has been achieved.

And how to know when this point has been reached? After all, since we all have different minds, there will be many different expressions of contemplation. The common thread that links them all is magic. When the heart sings as you enter the gate, when you are gladdened by the view of a new flower blooming, when you feel at peace and at home, you have found the magic that animates the mandala of the garden.

Magic is the common thread among all contemplative gardens.

Fruition

The Gardens

ほろほろと山吹ちるか滝の音

The Sound of Cherry Blossoms

During his wanderings, the eighteenth-century Japanese poet Matsuo Basho happened upon a waterfall. Watching the blossoms falling from nearby cherry trees and mixing with the cascading water at his feet, he composed a haiku:

> Waterfall
> Mountain entering in
> The sound of cherry blossoms

This garden was inspired by Basho's poem, in which the pink blooms and falling water become a single experience, a poet's vision of the universe. As you enter the garden through an ancient Japanese gate, pink and white roses presage the cherry blossoms further down the hill. Two kinds of bamboo are the soft background for shades of pink flowers. Madoke bamboo is used to make Japanese flutes, while the native Mesoamerican bamboo is from the jungles of Central America—a joining of East and West.

The place of arrival is the poet's hut. From here both the upper and lower falls are visible. This quiet refuge is partly shaded by a giant sycamore, and a Japanese black pine lends character and refinement.

1 Entrance   2 Steps   3 Mesoamerican Bamboo

4 Madoke Bamboo   5 Path   6 Viewing Deck

7 Flowering Cherry Trees   8 Large Waterfall

9 Poet's Hut   10 Anemones   11 Path   12 Forest

13 Giant Timber Bamboo   14 Viewing Deck

15 Upper Pond   16 Lower Pond   17 Cascades

18 Tree Ferns   19 Second Floor Patio   20 Lawn

21 Sycamore   22 Bamboo Fence   23 Timber Bamboo

24 House   25 Driveway   26 Samurai Gate

27 Rose Garden   28 Perennials   29 Viewing Stone

30 Laurel Tree   31 Swedish Ivy   32 Camellias

The
Adobe

The two active little daughters of the house love this garden. It is an organic extension of their home, filled with patios, open grassy areas, play spaces, and some hidden little gardens. There is even a tree house!

Instead of one open patio stretching across the front of the house, there are three, divided by walls of adobe designed to match the architecture. The first is a formal entryway in the old Spanish style. A fountain here is fed from a roof channel which spills dramatically over the stone at its base. The second patio area is for dining. Its walls are lower to take advantage of the view over the wide front lawn. The final patio area is informally arranged: from the kitchen, the children's sandbox and play area is in clear sight. The lawn is open for playing, and bordered by hedges of tall flowers.

A walkway made of old bricks leads down one side of the house, then out under an arbor toward the back lawn, where a pool is the focus of activity. Before reaching the lawn, an entrance through a low wall leads off this path and up into a small patio garden, where the adults can sit in the shade yet still hear the children. The garden gives room to grow: one day the girls may join their mother in tending the garden in the greenhouse, or riding in the Spanish riding ring at the far side of the garden.

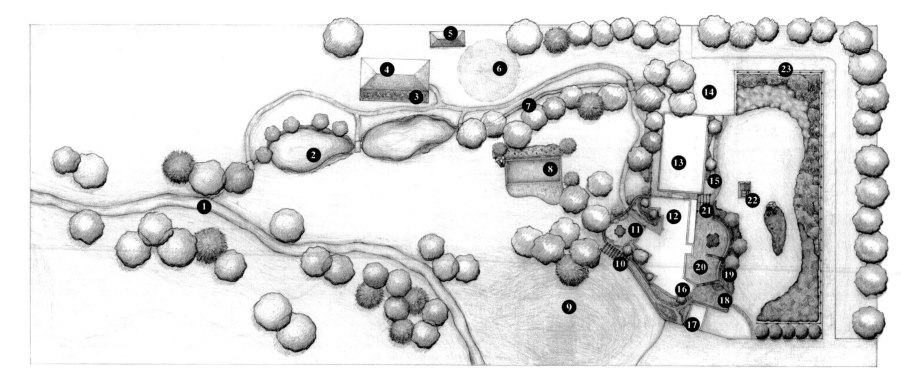

1 River   2 Ponds   3 Rose Garden   4 Greenhouse

5 Barn   6 Riding Ring   7 Ditch   8 Swimming Pool

9 Grass Tennis Court   10 Arbor   11 Back Patio

12 House   13 Guest Quarters   14 Parking Area

15 Sand Box   16 Front Entrance   17 Garage

18 Entry Patio   19 Water Fountain   20 Front Patio

21 Arbor   22 Play Set   23 Gravel Path

Flowers in Space

This contemplative space is a mandala composition consisting of nine mountains and three valleys. In the center is Mount Sumeru—the great Mother Mountain. She is adorned with a necklace of alpine flowers beneath a thousand tons of rock and dwarf pine trees. In her womb is a cave which looks at the peak of Dragon Mountain.

Dragon Mountain is one of the four animal spirits that surround the valley of water. From his mouth, water gushes forth, ending in a ten foot cascade at the foot of the Ceremony House. Opposite the dragon is the Snow Lion, with a white peak of dwarf pussytoes. A pathway hugs the river flowing down the mountain and leads to the bridge to Turtle Island, at the base of Turtle Mountain. From the island, one crosses the granite bridge to the Ceremony House, which is protected by the tall pine trees of Phoenix Mountain.

Four other mountains surround Mother Mountain, each a different color and possessing a different Buddha energy. At the base of Mount Sumeru is a green valley. This lies beneath Blue Mountain and the guest house. One exits the house onto a large patio which overlooks a granite monolith floating in a pond coated with pure cobalt. The line of water flowing through the carved stone leads the eye to the head of Dragon Mountain and the stream of water flowing from the Dragon's mouth. The energy of Blue Mountain is celestial, thus the color of the Sky.

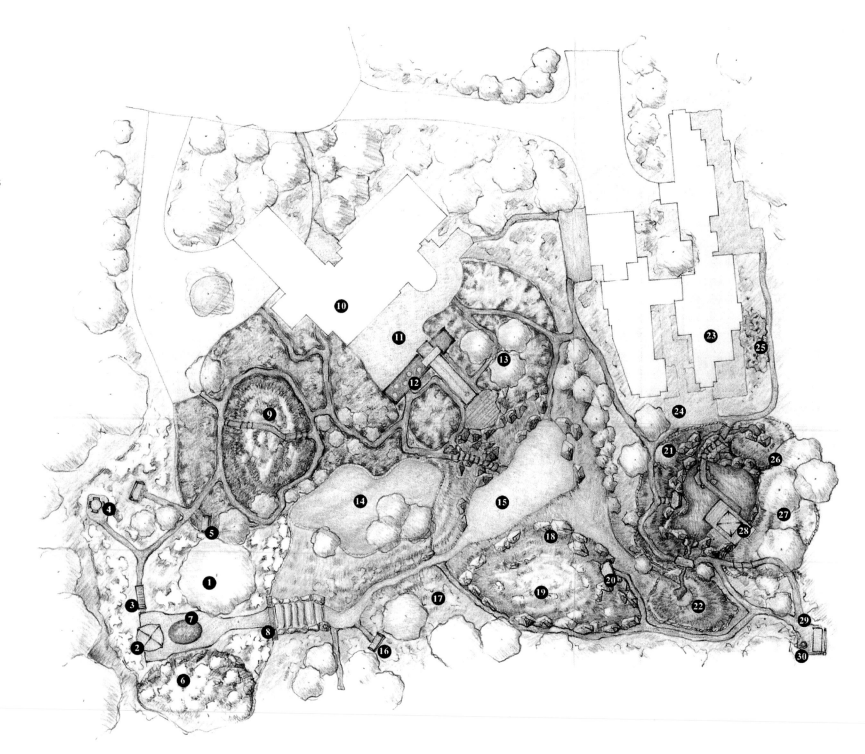

1 Garden of Western Paradise   2 Shrine   3 Bridge   4 Dinning Area   5 Lovers' Bench   6 White Mountain   7 Pond and Fountain   8 Torii Gate

9 Red Mountain   10 Party House   11 Patio   12 Fountain and Pond   13 Blue Mountain   14 Green Mesa   15 Green Meadow   16 Bench

17 Yellow Mountain   18 Alpine Garden   19 Mount Sumeru   20 Cave Entrance   21 Turtle Mountain   22 Dragon Mountain   23 Residence

24 Patio   25 Rose Garden   26 Snow Lion Mountain   27 Phoenix Mountain   28 Teahouse   29 Tsubo Niwa   30 Tsukubai

One passes over stepping-stones in the blue pond to enter the garden of the Red Mountain. Pathways lead to secluded benches and stairs climb the mountain to a vantage point at the top with an excellent view of Mount Sumeru. The energy here is passionate, seductive, and romantic.

Red Mountain leads to White Mountain, lying to the west of Mount Sumeru and housing the shrine to Amitabha Buddha. Its qualities are precision, discriminating intellect, and purity. The keyhole windows of the shrine frame the torii gate, which in turn frames a view of Mount Sumeru. In this garden all paths are straight and all forms geometric. The path from the torii gate to the shrines is lined with fragrant white lilies.

Passing through the torii gate one encounters Yellow Mountain. A bench at the bottom of this mountain is surrounded by the richness of gold. Its quality is fruition and ripeness. Five golden apple trees anchor the garden. At the base of Yellow Mountain is another green valley which leads back to Mount Sumeru and the secondary pathway to the cave at its heart.

Garden of the Healing Stones

This was once a tennis court, but after several back surgeries the owner could no longer play the game. She asked for a garden to contain two stone sculptures created by Jay Markel and Martin Mosko. In the course of building, it became clear she also needed a place to heal, to find new direction and inspiration. The object became to place stones to magnetize this kind of energy in a peaceful, natural environment.

The sculptures were part of *The Wheel Garden,* a circular arrangement of pieces that included stones representing Earth, Air, Fire, Water, and the central Prayer Stone, which turns like a Tibetan prayer wheel. The client purchased the Fire and the Prayer stones, which were placed at either end of her garden to form the north-south axis of the mandala.

The energy of the garden flows with the river, from the waterfall in the north near Fire to the pond in the south near the Prayer Stone. The western entrance is lush and inviting, passing through daphnia and hostas, and under dwarf trees. The east sector of the garden is marked by a mountain of flowers, where changing colors appear with each season.

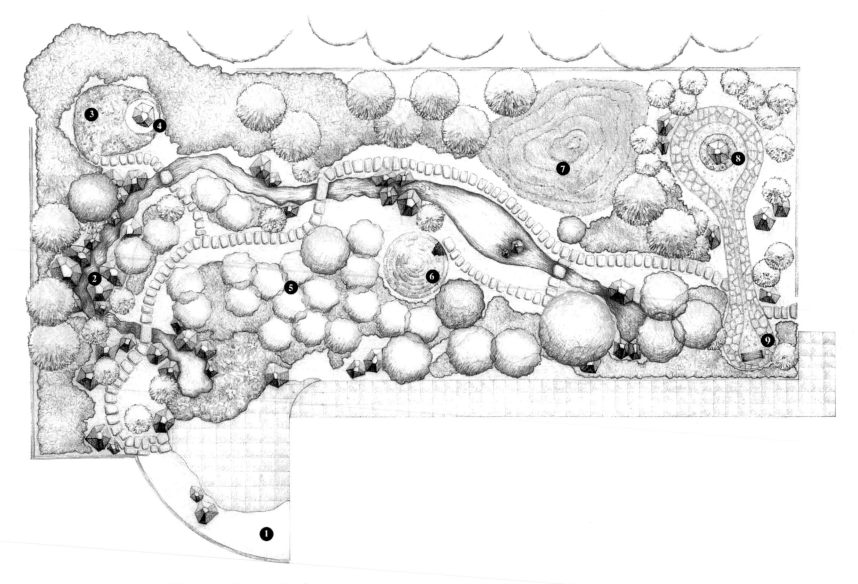

1 Entry Pathway   **2** Waterfall   **3** Meditation Garden
4 Fire Stone Sculpture   **5** Aspen Grove   **6** Shepherd
Hut   **7** Perennial Mountain   **8** Prayer Stone Sculpture
9 Bell and Bench

A Place to Fall In Love

This garden has transformed the entrance to the owner's home. Previously a cracked and frost-heaved asphalt drive took up this area. Now people are led on a journey through a wonderland of flowers on their way to the door.

The power of the long, curving path is obvious in this garden. Stone steps leading up from the drive lead onto a wooden bridge, which leads to stone steppers that meander through the length of the landscape. You can hear the waterfall before you can see it. Once across the bridge, its music tempts you away from the front door to admire its woodland setting and the array of colors that surround it. The river flows from the waterfall along the side of the house toward the door, and the path flirts with it, drawing closer and turning slightly away all along its course.

The back deck becomes an outdoor room for the owners through the spring and summer. The rest of the back garden has no formal paths, but anyone stepping off the deck is led along a swale of grass toward a mound of flowers. The natural movement is then toward a small bench set among trees and roses, a place to sit and fall in love.

1 Lantern   2 Bench   3 Perennial Garden   4 Deck

5 Hot Tub   6 Sculpture   7 Brick Patio   8 Bridge

9 Parking   10 Lawn   11 Bridge   12 Brook

13 Pathway   14 Headwaters   15 Entrance   16 Parking

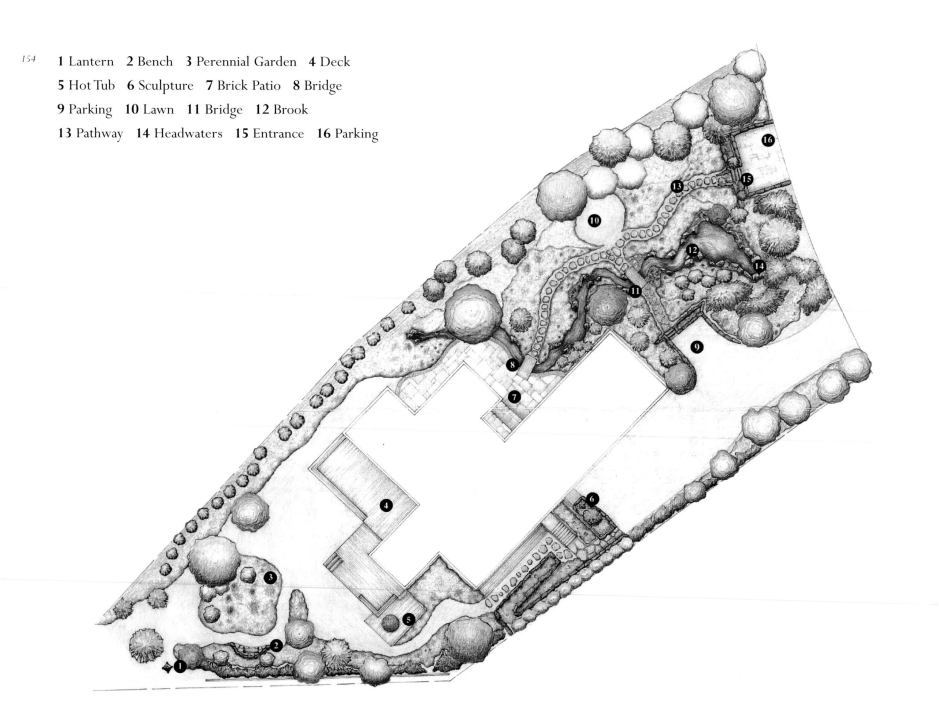

Notes and Photo Credits

158   The Ground

1 Susanne Fincher, *Creating Mandalas* (Boston: Shambhala Publications, 1991). 2 Donald Sander, M.D., *Navajo Symbols of Healing* (Rochester, VT: Healing Arts Press, 1979). 3 Tarthang Tulku, *Mandala Gardens* (Oakland: Dharma Publishing, 1991), p.55. 4 These three aspects of spirit are described in many religious traditions. The specifics of how each is understood varies, so we have used the broadest terms possible to describe them here.

The Path

Earth

1 Aniela Jaffe, "Symbolism and the Visual Arts," in *Jung, Man and His Symbols* (New York: Doubleday & Company, Inc.,1964), p. 232. 2 M. L. Von Franz, "The Process of Individuation," in *Jung, Man and His Symbols*, op. cit., p. 208–209. 3 Ibid., p. 210. 4 Jiro Takei and Marc P. Keane, *Sakuteiki: Visions of the Japanese Garden* (Boston: Tuttle Publishing, 2001), p.6. 5 Ibid., p. 183. 6 Ibid., p.185.

Water

1 Anthony Archer-Wills, *Designing Water Gardens: A Unique Approach* (London: Conran Octopus Ltd., 1999), p. 22. 2 Dawn Tucker Grinstain, *Pools, Ponds, and Waterways for Your Garden,* (New York: Grove Weidenfeld, 1992), p. 12. 3 George Plumptre, *The Water Garden* (London: Thames and Hudson Ltd., 1993), p. 27. 4 Ibid., p.14. 5 Ibid., p. 13. 6 Ibid., p. 57. 7 James van Sweden, *Gardening With Water* (New York: Random House, 1995), p. 26.

Fire

1 Marie-France Boyer, *Tree Talk: Memories, Myths, and Timeless Customs* (London: Thames & Hudson Ltd., 1996), pp. 14–16. 2 See, for example, Irini Rockwell, *The Five Wisdom Energies,* (Boston: Shambhala Publications, 2002). 3 Ibid., pp. 5–6. 4 Andrew Lawson, *The Gardener's Book of Color* (Pleasantville, NY: Reader's Digest Books, 1996), p. 24.

1 Jiro Takei and Marc P. Keane, *Sakuteiki: Visions of the Japanese Garden* (Boston: Tuttle Publishing, 2001), p. 61 et. seq. 2 Ibid. 3 Andrew Weil, M.D., *Health and Healing* (New York: Houghton Mifflin Company, 1995), p. 151. 4 Kenneth S. Cohen, *The Way of Qigong: The Art and Science of Chinese Energy Healing* (New York: Ballantine Books, 1997), p. 31. 5 Gary Zukav, *The Dancing Wu Li Masters: An Overview of the New Physics* (New York, Bantam Books, 1979), p. 48.

Space

1 Gero von Boehm, *Conversations with I. M. Pei: Light Is the Key* (New York: Prestel, 2000), p. 45. 2 Leonard Shlain, *Art & Physics: Parallel Visions in Space, Time, & Light* (New York: William Morrow and Company, Inc., 1991), p. 161. 3 Sidney Perkowitz, *Empire of Light: A History of Discovery in Science and Art* (New York: Henry Holt and Company, Inc., 1996), p. 6. 4 Gero von Boehm, op. cit., p. 38. 5 Craig Adcock, *James Turrell: The Light of Light and Space* (Berkeley: University of California Press, 1990), p. 36.

Photo Credits

The "weathermark" identifies this book as a production of Weatherhill, publishers of fine books on Asia and the Pacific. Editorial supervision: Ray Furse. Book and cover design: Liz Trovato. Proofreading: Mike Ashby. Production supervision: Bill Rose.